I am a whole load of nothing

And other heart-warming tales

Tom Sinclair

© 2015 Tom Sinclair
International Word Bank
London UK-Hollywood
ISBN: 978-0-9963927-2-3

Cover Photo by
Laurie Poole
LPhotography UK

This is a work of fiction. Any similarity to personalities living or dead is purely coincidental and exists only in the reader's mind.

Copyright 2015 by Tom Sinclair

All rights reserved. No part of this publication may be reproduced, distributed, or transmitted in any form or by any means including photocopying, recording or other electronic or mechanical methods without prior written permission of the publisher, except in the case of brief quotations embodied in critical reviews and certain other non-commercial uses permitted by copyright law.

For any information please contact
Baxter Daniels Ink Press
Internationalwordbank@gmail.com

ISBN: 978-0-9963927-2-3

© 2015 Tom Sinclair
Printed in the United States Of America
2015

Contents

This dirty old bastard 1
Tangents 5
Streatham High Street 9
Low to High 12
Three little words 18
30p holiday 25
(THE) 28
I am not in this 31
They 34
The view 36
Worm 38
Whisper 40
I am a whole load of nothing 42
A collection of nights 46
Lost in the hertz 50
Mushroom Tea 54
Let you in 58
Creep 63
Other heart-warming tales 67
I'm playing an out of tune piano with broken
strings and half the keys 70
These blue chains 76
Hometown 79

This dirty old bastard

Walking past the Ann Summers vibrator box, I noticed the sale sticker

Kicking the packaging I realised it was light, my toe silently agreeing it was probably a good buy

Up a bit further I noticed a packet of American Beef jerky,

I wondered if the two belonged together? Sounded like a good night

One that this dirty old bastard felt like he had missed out on

The best thing I ever learnt was that my feet and the shit for brains

That will swill around up there and counts as my conscience can and do act independently

And often move in two completely different directions

That first spring night I had one of the most morbid fantasies I've ever had

I had it while walking, I wasn't surprised, it's one of the things that will still get my heart pumping

I fucking hate and love the word inappropriate, it seals good thoughts away, it makes you hard

And then when you're just about to be getting some it makes you as soft as margarine

I thought if I find a women who wants to be tied up, I'd let her man come in the room and if he even

Looks at her I'll nearly kill the bastard, then we'd dump him somewhere like a forest or a ditch

Mind you there's nothing crazier than a man who actually loves his own woman

Poor bastards I know, I've been there, nothing worse than being at the mercy of another's madness

I've never slept with a women who wasn't some kind of crazed sociopathic bitch

They're my favourites of course, they're the ones that break my heart the best way

They either sledgehammer it into dust, or place a hand grenade in my chest and run for cover

They do it properly so I should never be stupid enough to fall for them again, even though I do

I think I met a sane woman once, best fuck I ever had, she has this dirty old bastards heart now

Of course she's not so fucking stupid to actually use it, but I hope she gets it out and looks at it

Like an exercise machine thick with dust, she likes to know it's hers and no-one else has use of it

It's good to know it's somewhere else, then I don't have to worry about it. So I like losing things now,

Because I know those things are going to end up in a pair of safer hands than mine

I've torn inwards at myself, I once held a shit in for 5 days, talk about possessive

The next 6 months I had to work really hard at not shitting myself all the time

It's true, if you try to hold onto anything to hard it'll fuck you over

So she's welcome to this dirty old bastards heart

This way I'm free to look at twenty year old girls

I don't have to worry about falling in love

Feeling in love is overrated

Trust me I've tried it

I've been married once, I used to be nice

Dirty old bastard suits me better

Like a glove

Filled with other peoples tears

I think the kindest thing that a woman ever did for me

Is when the paper lady in the hospital, paid for me to have a paper with her own money

Me a grown man vomiting, crying then vomiting again for 4 days with a drip in his arm

So, so pathetic, love has cost me enough already, now I only like reading stories about it

I will read about other people feeling in it, and someday I might tell myself "that used to me"

…someday

Tangents

Blankly it hits me

That the simple truth

That one day this sonofabitch will die

That time peels away like the skin of a tangerine

Then the bitch of the world eats each segment

The juice of our lives runs in the streets

Can you feel it?

The palpable decay of your life

The drip, drip, into the gutter

Now I don't mean to get all depressive and stuff

But isn't this poetry?

Isn't it?

Probably not

I've not been bothered to rhyme

For quite some time

Get it?

Shit I broke my run

Just for the sake of a pun

And at that a bad one

I'm fed up of restrictions in Art

Shouldn't this be where we play?

Were we are at our freemost? Freeist?

Apparently neither of those are words according to Word

Our time to explain how we feel

Who we are

And to stem the tide

Of the drip, drips

And all the lies

The stink

Oh one day I'll sell out

I'll say yes, yes

Instead of no

But I will have to be saying something somebody will want to buy for that to happen

Not just slapping my peers across the cheek

They need it

I AM A WHOLE LOAD OF NOTHING

I need it

I'd rather somebody fought me openly

Than kissed my arse

Never kiss my arse

Nothing against arse kissing

But trust me its filthy in there

I throw away pants rather than suffer the indignity of them being washed

By my mother

Sorry mum

Especially since she buys me the replacements

I was never made to appease

Maybe to please

If I make someone laugh

It feels all warm

Alleviates the ache inside

I'd rather take a knife to my own throat

Than anyone else's

My flesh is my own

To mark

To dig into

To make bleed

The two scars on my left fist

From where I punched the wall in the mental ward until I lost the skin

I like them

It shows my inability to give in

My ability to carry on fighting even if it's with myself

That's always the best fight

One I get up to in the morning

If I get up

Streatham High Street

Muffin top overflows

Green trousers

A pram is pushed

A pair of married beggars stops

Need food, need money

This is my wife

I'll buy you food

Don't understand, little English

Just a pound

I move on apologising

He relents

Wide street full of cars

A man carries keys, lunch

And three invoice pads

The shop I'm waiting for

To buy things I can't eat

Another guy returns as he opens

TOM SINCLAIR

The shop is as good

As his word

The man who runs it

Is pudgy and animated

With glasses that tell of our shared interest

Afterwards

I make my way towards a bus stop

The first restaurant I find isn't serving,

Later I turn a corner and find myself

In a world of Somalian cafés

No menus

Nobody's eating

Nobody's drinking

They watch TV in silence

Outside they chat with excitement

I eat elsewhere

Not wanting to disturb their peace

I read a Christmas card from my Chaplin Mirabel, smile and eat without

Saying grace

I ask for a fork for my chips, drink my pineapple soda

Wish I knew a way to divide my food

I AM A WHOLE LOAD OF NOTHING

Feed the hungry

But I have to make do with eating my burger with my hands

And knowing my father would not be

Well pleased

I stole the pen I wrote this with

It was a pound for the paper

But I cannot buy my peace

I will have to fight for that

Carve freedom,

without even a plastic knife

Low to High

It's been a strange couple of weeks

I've been spending my time

Drinking with a homeless guy, daytime stuff

Trying on petty alcoholism for size

His names Sully

Fresh out of Chelmsford

12 months - Assault

He head-butted a police officer

He has a certain style

He pretends to be racist

But I don't buy it, or I don't want too

I know another guy who does that

He's a triple figures

And despite pretending to be total cunt he's alright too

First day I met Sully

He took me to a pub

Brought us both drinks

I said to him

"This aint right

You need that money"

But I still drunk mine

And he brought us another

I drunk that too

I said "I'll buy them on Monday"

As he shared his stolen

Scotch eggs with me

And free things do taste better

We both agreed

As we salted the eggs with the pub's shakers

And I shared my laughter with him

The day after the next

I meet him for lunch

And some cold cans

And I level with him

"You never asked me what I do Sully?"

"It's none of my business"

Chest out, "I'm a writer"

Translation - unemployed

"Do you mind if I write about you? "

"Not really, I don't read much"

A couple of days later I wanted to take him for a warm lunch,

But he didn't fancy it...

I didn't feel I could drink

I had group therapy, so I think he could sense my reluctance

"He said what AA?" and we laughed

He had the Sunshine, and Gazza, Al

And Irish Jimmy with his blister - who I liked the most - he had style

I liked the way he told stories and jokes

And even the way he squeezed your arm when he got to the point

Or the punchline

He came back from the Tesco metro with a bottle of white wine in his trouser pocket

And shared it with everyone, well anyone who wanted some

Take a hit

Take a hit

Sully sleeps now under an overhang in a sleeping bag on the rocks

I think about him when I rains

I could be him

He could be me

I AM A WHOLE LOAD OF NOTHING

A learned friend of mine said

After a while you realise all we really have is our commonality

I was out the next night at Micks house party

He was breaking out the weekend drugs supply

Him and his work colleagues

Were really going through it

He asked for a financial contribution

They didn't oblige - cunts I thought

At least I didn't partake

Brought my own booze

And eggs and bread for everyone breakfast

(Unfortunately Mick doesn't eat eggs, but I suspect he doesn't eat)

I said to Mick

"You live like a homeless person"

And

"I've never seen you eat"

I realise my prejudice

But everyone is

Some shade of Arsehole

The worse ones don't know it yet

"Karma is a piece of shit"

I said the words came out angry

Angrier than I expected

One of the non-chipping in Cunts

Said

"I try and live by the idea of karma"

Now I realise

He is probably failing

We all probably are

Still the morning sunrise view

Out of Micks high rise apartment

Is amazing

Maybe it's worth the cunt-ish

Work colleagues

With their misunderstanding of karma

The poor and the destitute

They get it

It's sharing what you can spare

I missed it but a guy in a wheelchair

Wheeled right over to Al

And gave

Him a four pack

And a fiver

I AM A WHOLE LOAD OF NOTHING

Things were looking up for Al

That day

They know that this day is the only

Day that matters

Everything else is daydreams, religion

And politics

There is a lot of poetry in people

It's easier to hear it

When you're closer

To the ground

If you like

Nearer rock bottom

Three little words

Not what you think

Because some words

Are now too hard to say

Not that I don't want to say them

I can't

Not I won't

Because I may

Break this unspoken feeling

This sugar coated sweetness

And I can't lose you

Not yet

Maybe not ever

Because parts of me are broken

In all new and uninteresting ways

But to you I'm new and interesting

I AM A WHOLE LOAD OF NOTHING

Not the record on repeat

Scratched at the word

De, De, De, feat

Because it still feels a feat to see

Your feet

And I like them

And don't want to hear them

Run the other way

I can't let you do that

Not yet

Maybe not ever

The last girl I said…

No I don't want to talk about

My string of romantic defeats

Because I still hope

In my own dark way

I'll win one yet

That you'll come running

Out of the crowd

And I'm bloody, broken, but not bowed

And I'll see you and the press will crush around and my manager

Will towel my brow

And I'll mouth three words at you

Because you can't hear me above

The crowd and I don't need you to

Because you can lip read

I hope you can mind read

That when I say

See you soon

Can you hear the subtext?

See through my bluff

Read behind the lies

Through my eyes

That the three little words

I can't say

Because I don't want to lose you

Not yet

Maybe never

Are maybe

Don't hurt me

I AM A WHOLE LOAD OF NOTHING

Just because I'm broken

Doesn't mean I'm comfortable

With breaking in a different way

It took a long time to stick

This mask back together

Make it smile

Let it cry

I'm not emotionally retarded

I'm intellectually guarding

The part of me most at odds with me

That most fickle bit of me

My brain

Chemically imbalanced

Capable of momentary glimpses

Of pure MDMA happiness

And troughs months long

Of insane unhappiness

See I know your last boyfriend

He was bipolar like me

Because I know you need to see

That I'm more than a shared condition

With your past

I respect this will take time

And I call you beautiful

You call me darling

And my fingers are crossed

That this is enough

I don't want to get sentimental

And start declaring undying things

Because everything either changes

Or dies

I don't want to risk what we have

On a muscle

Because it's got just one job

And that's to keep me alive long enough to see you by my deathbed

looking into your eyes before I die

And I'll want to say something profound like

"Rosebud"

But instead I'll squeeze your hand

And say

See you there

I AM A WHOLE LOAD OF NOTHING

And it will have to do

Because I want you to outlive me

And do the fuck you want

Because I'm an overweight poet

With a life shortening mental position

So all I can promise

Isn't enough

But it's all I've got

A collection of worn out parts

But their yours if you want them

Besides

I give a good foot massage

And I'm not a bad cook

So I hope it'll do

Because I'm not just crazy

I'm crazy about you

It's all insanity

But I'm ok with that

Because I have to be

But you don't

Just because the showman gives

You the key

It doesn't mean you have to take them

I'm enjoying our extended test drive

So, I'm just putting it out there

And if it's not too much to ask

If it's really ok then

Kiss me quick, or fuck me hard, Take your pick

30p holiday

This is it, no pre-booking required
I change a milk stealer coin in the
Automated machine provided
My brass Margaret is divided
Into her constituent circles and
Pentagons, I insert one of each
Into the turn style, it gives into my
Weight and begrudgingly accepts
My passage into the departure lounge

I am given a selection of seats
Within private booths, I select
Mine carefully considering
Presence of inflight paper
Lack of socially disturbing
Holes, presence of coat hook.
I enter my cubicle

And I place my bag and

Coat on the hook like so

Trousers down around

My ankles, bottom on

Freshly wiped around seat,

The complete package

I shut my eyes and I am

Away on distant lands

In caravans, laser beams

Dig through mobile homes

My friend turns up, smiles

Cups my balls and is gone

The caravan swings under

The weight of me, I am

Lost in a sea side town

The beach dust lingers

On my tongue, the

Taste of non-human salt

This world slips and slides

Dreams within dreamscapes

I AM A WHOLE LOAD OF NOTHING

My mind envelops

Me and protects me

From the mundane

In here I am hero, I am

Villain, and heroine, and

Simultaneously I am nothing

Just a passenger of wild reeling thought

As I leave the arrival zone I pick up a meal

Discarded in a takeaway bag on the hand dryer

(THE)

Days are longer

Than the night now

Blackened bars

AND neon signs

Prop inside my MIND

The SUN

Is for families

Shining Examples

Of GOD's plan

Twilight Roams

From within

The ONLY thing that

Twists more than my *mind*

IS a GO-GO dancer ON stage

Save me from Packaged holidays

And FAKED Tans

I AM A WHOLE LOAD OF NOTHING

Join me in *Heathen* WAYS

The only sacrament

Is JOY through companionship

I prefer

My company

In small doses

Like a graveyard

I rust, pitted and discoloured

And flake like snow

Adrift of emotion

IF language is infinite in combination

Why do so MANY sing the SAME song?

I listen to Tom **Waits**

LEADBELLY

Jim Morrison

And Kurt **Cobain**

Men with something to SAY

WITHOUT THAT

Sway to the middle ground

That erosion of soul

As we all eventually

FALL

Into <u>obscurity</u>

Pour us a drink

We're going to need it today

FAST

I scratch my SONG

Into grammatically questionable poems

And onto toilet doors

I bleed with me

I'm full of myself

I know who I'll miss when they're gone

And it **ISN'T** me

Life isn't Monopoly it's more Russian roulette

One day someone will put the right person in charge

Then someone will invariably kill them

Like Abe, J.F.K, Boudicca

In the END we are all

Blood <u>and</u> *dust*

And Oliver Reed,

well

<u>He knew</u>

I am not in this

It is devoid of me

And I am devoid of it

Or am I just devoid?

I am absent

In my absence

We will both look for me

Between these lines

But I will not be present

In my own presence

Don't meet my gaze

For I'm not looking at anything

I'm remembering Plath and Hemmingway

And I wonder if this void

Is something we all have in common?

A space to fill with words

But I have no stomach for it today

The blanks are filled

With yet more blanks

Who will think like me when I am gone?

If you are reading the original hand written version

Please burn after reading

Cremate my sentences

Sacrifice this text

Everything dies

Apart from ideas

The insistence of knowledge

Socrates dared to not know it all

It is the gaps that spur me on

Or they would

If I was here

But I am not

I am a sequence of events to never be repeated

I pray it is never to be repeated

All our fates shall be different for vanities sake

We all have blanks waiting to be filled

My glass is neither empty nor full

It is simply – gone

Do you know where?

Would you tell me?

If you were here, where I am now

Even if it risked your own salvation?

...Don't lie to me

Even if I'm not here, one day I may hear it on the summer's breeze

One day I may be there, standing in your spot

And you maybe back here, where I am now.

I would hope I would treat you kindly

Wouldn't you hope that too?

Even if you're here yet, one day you may be here

Devoid of yourself, devoid of life

Just devoid

They

All eat your heart

Some of them swallow it whole

Blink and its gone

Others nibble chew and spit

Making faces when it doesn't taste

'Nice'

Others slow cook it for weeks

Then when it comes to the eating of it

They feed it to the dog

Some like to dry it out

Like washing on a line

And occasionally spit on it

To keep you in line

I AM A WHOLE LOAD OF NOTHING

Some forget they have it at all

And it goes both limp and rotten

From sheer stupid neglect

I like mine cooked medium rare

I like mine to have a little fight left in it still

But then I've always been a carnivore

And its only really muscle

Another cut in the butchers window

But you should always honour

Their sacrifice and eat every little last bit

The view

Would have been different if I looked out of the window

But I didn't want to

I had everything I needed at that moment within reach

The taste of your lips lingering

My mouth firmly around the back of your neck

I'm not sure if you wanted me to do that more than I did

I felt the desire was strongly mutual

I wanted to tattoo your body with my teeth

And run great welts down your back

I can still imagine my fingers deep inside you

When you circled your clit to orgasm

One final climax

I can remember three

All were different, all were intense

I think you might have been napping

Whilst I traced my finger over the contours of your face

I AM A WHOLE LOAD OF NOTHING

Much more unique than any landscape

And after I'd explored those untamed lands

I kissed your sleeping lips awake

Because part of me was afraid

That your momentary dream

Would become the true reality

And I would lose this, my own dream forever

Worm

Sectioned anatomy,

Little space from brain to stomach.

Strength in simplicity,

Basic needs – minimal stimulus,

Few obstacles stand in its way.

The boy digs with his hands in the black soil.

He finds the worm and upturns its living grave.

Today is halfway through the day, the worm wriggles away

The boy grabs a nearby stick,

Brandished as a scientific instrument,

Showing little compassion

Which suggests he will likely, repeat this again in the future.

With patience as a state of mind he toys with his prey.

Spearing the worm he is overcome with many ways to express learned-mind states.

His mother appears blonde haired, with a wry smile.

"Has your brother being putting ideas in your head?

Come back tomorrow."

The boy flicks the stick, the worm wounded wriggles free.

He is no longer one of lives perfections.

But he is free.

Whisper

There is violence within your silence

A whisper between the sheets

And sighs between your thighs

I take you again

I am hard outside

You are soft inside

I know I frustrate you

Everywhere but the bedroom

With my crap jokes

And poor etiquette

And tendency to rub

People the wrong way

I will continue to rub you

Continue to please you

As it pleases me too

Please you

You accuse me of being a feminist

I AM A WHOLE LOAD OF NOTHING

I answer the slur with an

Orgasm for each of us

I'm an egalitarian

I reaffirm

But I do not mind being

A feminist pawn

After all it is with the Queens gambit

That I most often reach checkmate

I am a whole load of nothing

I knew that the moment I let the jealousy rise in me

The moment I put Ego in front of friendship

I smelt my own stink

Undoing myself

So everyone could see my pins disassemble

Just a child pretending to be deep

Playing with words

Pushing them around pages

Like the monkey looking for Shakespeare

There is such music in self-spun lies

The Orchestra of my pomposity

The jazz of my gypsy heart

The blues of my own unmaking

My Rome will fall

It'll crash around

My ankles

When you come and call

I AM A WHOLE LOAD OF NOTHING

Though you won't call

Not on me

Because I've got a whole load of nothing

Waiting on me

A wide catalogue of fuck ups

Sitting on my coach

One slides over

And whispers in my ear

"Do you remember…"

And I nod

"Do you remember…"

I nod again

"And how about"

And I nod once more

Then a single tear forms

From a single duct

And the ghosts of my failures

Gather, huddle and laugh

The joke is on me, and me, and me

And my past stretches out into infinity

Flattening me out

Stretching me

Beyond capacity

And I wait

And wait

For the executioner to come

Then a man in a suit and tie

Tips his bowler hat

And he says there are

Penalties for being a prat

But we deal with them

With Bureaucratic

Efficiency

And he inserts his umbrella

Into my rectal cavity

And opens it up as if for a heavy shower

Tearing me fully asunder

Into pure whisky tears laced with regrets

When I feel the thunder

And paranoid with fears

I don't trust

Some people

Because they are stranger than they allow themselves to be

Me I'm probably more ordinary

I AM A WHOLE LOAD OF NOTHING

Than fate would allow

I'm probably done aggrandising

My insecurities

For a while

For a while

Come sit with me a while

Because I don't have a lot of somethings

And I value your time

It's all we really have

That's actually ours

If I was a lot richer

I'd spend it in bars

But being an alcoholic

Requires focus and commitment

So I'm being something else

A voyeur at life

Come watch the sky fall into black

Hold my hand for a while, smile then run the knife down my back

A collection of nights

The best friends in high heels

To the well-dressed woman

In blue matching outfit

With a boob freely

Hanging

I've drunk

Cider and smoked

Other peoples cigarettes

And the one armed man

Hustling people for 20ps

'I'm a genuine cripple!'

He exclaims

Stump exposed

No one stumps up

Or the gypsy bands

Who do better

With Joviality

And the young Asian man

Spitting sick

In strings

Like dewy spider webs

I let one woman squeeze

Behind me in the barriers

But she's not close enough and her

Bag gets stuck

Nights fall into each other

A collection of the worn

And the beautiful

I heave! Ho!

Between

Feeling switched on

To feeling numb

I love the mix

The mixing

London

Is multi toned

Wickedly diverse

But I still like girls with

Thick thighs and thicker eyebrows the best

With country accents

And a hesitance at lives

Carousel

We spin

Like tops

And collapse

In heaps

And I love the marionettes

That surround me

I love their ragged lives

And misshapen hearts

It's my capital city

And I wouldn't have it any other way

Headphones

And mobile phones

Rucksacks

And butt cracks

How can I love anyone else

I'm a part of my city

Somebody asks me if I would

Ever teach?

I say no

I AM A WHOLE LOAD OF NOTHING

Because

I'm still learning

The different chicken shop perfumes

And the rhythm of urban life

It's a rhumba without end

And I watch it's curves

I swallow it's pill

The streets are my medicine

A million lives here

Another million there

It's a shanty of lives

And I click my fingers

To the four four

Or the foxtrot

It's my home

I'm at home

In its madhouse

The only way I live is by

Stepping back

And watching the mayhem

It has such sights to show me still

Lost in the hertz

Somehow in the data

Archived on a lone floppy disk

I exist

As a digital smear

On the randomly accessed memories of our past

Somewhere in the mass store

I must be backed up

Too poor to corrupt

But am I more than a worn mechanism?

Stillborn into pure digital

We are all noughts

To someone else's ones

Do you caress the moulded plastic?

Whisper sweet nothings,

To your latest hard driver?

Or would you upload,

Your old lust,

Onto my trusted server?

Down In the IO flow

I'm lost in the shifting bits

Until I pause at your logic gates

Stopping to change compact disc

Will you remember to archive,

This love-bytten last kiss?

Don't delete this conversation

Until you've remembered

Your password

(It's the name of your first Tamagotchi)

Sad how everything gets so compressed

No room for redundancy

In this system of ours

If you can't make the upgrade path

They won't let you install the latest updates

And you'll miss the double click

It's not that life processes too fast

More that we forget we can slowdown

Clocks run on quartz

So please mix a little silicon in with my oxygen

The internet told me that Feldspar contains nothing but and/ore

And we are but shadows in devices

Specs of time, lost in the hertz

Remember that nothing is forever

Data-farms rise and fall

Do you really think

This can last forever?

And I thought us poets where the fools?

Come embrace me my lover

We don't have to say it out loud

Otherwise it might reach up to the cloud

Yes remember sweet Caroline

She kissed me on tip-toes

And later I danced with my wife in the kitchen

Before she had it bypassed

Cocktails for dinner

In a nitrogen bath

Enough browsing my history

It's nearly time to end this session

And run system checks

Seems I've got a virus or two

I'll try and keep them away from my

Handshaking protocol

I AM A WHOLE LOAD OF NOTHING

Though they remind me of you, my sweet Dos 6.2

We've not come as far

As some like to think

So give me a bar

And an iced cool drink

One for the highway

Before I catch the last data bus

I think I'm disassembling into hex

Can you reassemble the code

And defrag me once again?

I think I'm still human

But I like it when you give me a debug

Please kind USERNAME, tonight let's forget the write protect

Mushroom Tea

Is it me?

Or does this tea

Taste

A little mushroomy

Like a cheesy pint

Somethings

Not quite right

With how

This

Reality

Is appearing to me

Are the rich

Getting richer?

And the poor

Getting poorer?

It's now not seen as fair

I AM A WHOLE LOAD OF NOTHING

To be asking for morer

If you're not the 1%

We don't care to the factor of 99%

Stop demanding equilibrium

It's your medical delirium

We've found your place

Now sign your rights away

If you get hungry

Go to the local food bank

We've given all your money

To my mates corrupt, bankrupt

Freshly back in business bank

Now don't get me wrong

I see your point of view

In the rear view

Of my 2nd Mercedes too

But austerity

Needs your sacrifice

To succeed

Got to pull up

All the unwanted weeds

I'm a lyrical gardener

On Question time

Give all my answers

In perfect rhyme

But only dear listeners

If you share your thyme

Because even with a 10% raise

My salaries truly a crime

So if society is truly to benefit

We must slash the money

That we give to those on benefits

Take from the poorest

To top up the

Parliamentary pensions

Owning three properties

Is dreadfully expensive

My expenses barely cover two

And if I had more than two babies

I swear I'd smother them

I put down my tea

And splash my face in cold water

I AM A WHOLE LOAD OF NOTHING

I have a nap

Wake up a few hours later

Switch on the TV

Tune in the radio

Read todays paper

Fuck me it was all real

Not a hallucination

Or a seizure

This worlds more frakked

Than a frakkin

Exploratory shoal gas drilling mission

END

OF

TRANSMISSION

Let you in

To the forgotten apologies

The dimpled thighs

And the bedroom sighs

I write one

To

One

Listen to the words

Falling like autumn

I'm mean

With my meaningless

Meanings

And see my flowless

Flow-ing

Flow

Lost with twin luggage

I'm set to depart

In a room

I AM A WHOLE LOAD OF NOTHING

Full of objects on standby

Melting the polar ice caps

A little bit more

I write my trashy words

In the Trashy bedsit

I pine for

Waiting to be trashed

If only somebody would take notice

And sue me

That would be OK

Still I whine for tarts

In tartan to reject me

Batter my consciousness

Into unconsciousness

I want to leave The city

I want to leave The Dungeon

But they only made one and a half

Bits of my eight bit life

I need more memory

For my memories

I want to slide all

My past into the dustbin

Apart from you

I will cradle you

Like a misguided parent

I will play peekaboo

With my recollections

Until the tape breaks

But when you shoplift

From the garage

I will conveniently *erase*

Your number plate

Shrug my shoulders

Wave goodbye

Because my dreams

Are within dreams

And your streams

Are inside me

Your water is my water

And it's sacred

People are sacred

It's not idolatry

I AM A WHOLE LOAD OF NOTHING

It's a fact

Like ancient temples

In deserts

We will be dynamited

And some will weep

Some will not

No grief can ever be universal

Because no-ones compassion

Or empathy can be complete

We are not made that way

No-one can be that way

Religion is a well thought out fantasy

Based on a white lie

But God is great

If you accept the possibility

Of nothing you must comprehend

The plausibility of a plan

So take me to the promised land

As long as it has USB charging sockets

Netflix, wifi and comfortable sofa's

Else send me to Hell and I will

Spend eternity finding the burnt souls

Of the people I longed to meet

But died before I found my feet

Drinking pennyroyal tea with Kurt

Smoking heroin with Winehouse

Pot with Marley

And me and Bukowski will drink, spit and fight over women who don't want either of us

Not tonight

Read me no poetry

Sing me no songs

Hum the theme tune

To that advert we both like

Save the money

Forget the tombstone

Send my ashes into the sky

Spare your words

But not your tears

Silence is the best thing

After all our years

Creep

I don't belong here

I'm no hero, never have been

I have no white horse

Besides I can't ride

I know

I've tried

Looks there goes Beowulf

He looks like he can hold his beer

Voiced by that Sexy Beast

Ray Winstone

I'm nobody

But with the risk

Of sounding like Stallone

(It's Brando, I now know)

"I could have been a contender"

Well in my dreams, I could

So I'll write about my lonely days

I'll also write about my really happy ones

And you'll never know I exist

I will be the whisper in the mist

I probably live down your street

I'm the boy that won't make eye contact

I'll never slay your dragons

Because I'm never done with my own

Whatever the fuck happened to Radiohead?

Wherever did Thom Yorke fuck off too?

They never catch the real ones

Because they are wise enough

Not to believe their own lies

Their beautiful lies

Like myths

Spoon fed with happiness

Dry dripped success

I know I'm a loser baby

I know this world will kill me

And if God exists

I AM A WHOLE LOAD OF NOTHING

I hope he laughs

And I hope he is a Viking

And we can share beer

And stories of lost loves

And won battles

The key to victory

Is knowing that you've won

Whether you do that with

Your swords

Your pen

Or with your dick in your hands

Die with a smile

Enjoy making Odin the all father wait a bit longer

I don't want to die in my bed

Maybe somebody else's

That sounds like more fun

Somebody to weep over me

Or bury me in a forest

An unmarked grave

For an unremarkable life

Who am I kidding?

I want an army of professional mourners

A twenty gun salute

Even though I was never in the army

(But I was a boy scout and an air cadet briefly and that counts still right?)

And I want Thom Yorke

To come out of retirement

And play my funeral

I want

Fake plastic trees, Karma police, Creep

And I want president Obama to make a speech

About how he read my novel and cried the whole way through

And he never realised a white dude could be a brother

And I want 50 Bulls to be sacrificed in my honour

But don't give me virgins in heaven

Give me a woman with plenty of brains, sass and arse

Who can speak French in the bedroom

It's not like I'm asking for much

Other heart-warming tales

Urban vampires

Sit under strip lighting

Her blue eyes lie

To me

Again

They shadow my shadows

And check the emails you haven't written me yet

When did love become

A 21st century

Reinvention?

We are commercially

Broken

But I'm not going

To waste more ink on the obvious

Flaws in this tumbleweed Utopia

I will miss you

When our continents shift

And when we split

While I've still got the taste of

You in my mouth

Though I can't be bitter

Because you were oh so sweet

I could lick all the crevices

Of your crevices

And run my hands over your dimpled thighs

Within my imagination

From our memories

Because If I am bereft of you

Then I hope that you

Feel this absence in you too

And that I'll miss our time differences

And your sober responses

To my drunken messages

I could never make you laugh

Not really

Although I often feel funny

When I wake up

I AM A WHOLE LOAD OF NOTHING

And you not there

Still

I realised that I've never taken a single photo of you

But I know your face

And it will always have its place

Because the story of me

Is filled with chapters of you

And I still finger your bookmark

And dog ear my favourite pages too

I'm playing an out of tune piano with broken strings and half the keys

If my life played like a jazz record

I couldn't bear to place the needle on the black

I wouldn't want to hear the melody

I like to think my life

Is a mystery off track

Too many people sing their song

Like it's written in stone

Like all the hard work has been and gone

But baby it's just begun

Light the candles

There's a blackout in my heart

I crawl the short distance

To my stomach

Sit in my acid

Play with my bile

But your absent from my gut

I AM A WHOLE LOAD OF NOTHING

I can't feel what you feel

But it is doesn't mean I haven't tried

Doesn't mean that I won't still

So if you decide that you can't love me

I'll do my best to understand

Sometimes the only hand that can take mine

Is mine

Remember if I sound out of tune

I'm playing an out of tune piano with broken strings and half the keys

Why don't you sit for a while

And try and play a duet with me

Think we might manage chopsticks

Which is ironic

Because Chinese is my least favourite cuisine

I've numbered all my song sheets

Highlighted the chorus

It goes like this;

I never know what I feel

I'll never know what you feel

Until it's too late to remember

How we ever sung our songs

But sing with me

All the same

I could write a verse about your eyes

I could write a song about your thighs

But I'm not given to sentimentality

Until it's too late to even matter

I like it when you brush your hair

Sweep it from side to side

I think I knew

When you told me where to stick it

That part of me would always be into you

I'd lie if I said you were too good for me

I'd lie if I said I was no good for you

Truth is we were perfect for each other

And that's a terrifying truth

Can you remember our chorus?

It goes like this;

I never know what I feel

I AM A WHOLE LOAD OF NOTHING

I'll never know what you feel

Until it's too late to remember

How we ever sung our songs

But sing with me

All the same

Life is a disease of the living

It doesn't curse those who die inside

If I said I'm not afraid of being dead

I'm part lying

I'm afraid of being forgotten

I'm afraid of all this not mattering

But you matter

I know this much to be true

I haven't wept for you yet

Because when I start I'll never stop

I'll flood the streets of London

So when you ask me what you mean to me

And the words I treasure all fail me so

Listen to the humming from below my throat

It goes like this;

I never know what I feel

I'll never know what you feel

Until it's too late to remember

How we ever sung our songs

But sing with me

All the same

When you stumbled on me in my ruins

When I took you in my arms

How could I know what I know now?

But some questions aren't worth the price of asking

Some words fall from our fingers

Never to linger on our lips

I won't sing our chorus one more time

Because the words don't quite matter

I feel as much as I can

If that can't be enough my love

Then can I ask you to take my hand?

I don't want anything but your warmth

And to feel your palm-print on my heart

Where it's belonged all along

I AM A WHOLE LOAD OF NOTHING

Maybe we all just long

To belong

So long

These blue chains

These chains aren't mine

But they fit me all the same

As I drag their weight behind me

They follow me true

Sometimes the blues chase me

Like whisky following beer

At all night piano bars on the Vegas strip

And even

If you say you love me

These feelings won't be chased away

Some of us are destined

For happiness

And others are destined

For a great deal

Of pain

I'll leave you on an open desert road

You can thumb a lift

I AM A WHOLE LOAD OF NOTHING

With an average guy

Put your bags into his car baby

And drive into the sunset together

Because it's all just dusk to me

I want you to be happy

I think one of us can make it

So please, let it be you

I don't want to bring you down

Not when you made me smile

I cannot escape me honey

But I bet you can

You can beat the odds

And I want you to

More than I ever wanted to

Save your tears for the next funeral

I'm doing this for you

People are just no good

No good to themselves

No good to one another

Just no good

See I want to spare you

From that no good part of me

And spare me

From the no good in you

And if you really do love me

You'll see all this is true

Knowing that this is true

Doesn't make me happy

But it does make me blue

And if your honest that's why you liked me

That's why you fell in love with me

That's why we're so fucked up

Because you can't be loved by a man

Whose in love with his own blues

I've always heard them sing to me

They've always been here for me

Unlike you my darling

Baby I've always got my chains of blue

Hometown

One armed checkout assistants

Like bandits of capitalism

Stick "it" up

Instead of "em"

Kids wearing jazzed up versions

Of the uniform you used to wear

The waft of shampoo in their hair

I used to be a dirty kid

Mind and body

Ate woodlice

Picked my nose

Jerking off incessantly

That old woman's stare at the fish counter

Stays with you, stays with

You

The way some woman walk

Swinging their bottom

Like it's the only way to walk

The only way they walk

Is maybe the only way

They walk

I've seen guys doing it and its fascinating

Like watching strippers

When you're a virgin

But it's not the real thing

YOU know it's not the real thing

Even when you're a virgin

But sometimes it's all you've got

Like hope, pocket change

Clean underwear

Here I am sitting drinking

People probably thinking I'm an misogynist

For saying what I'm thinking

Overhearing three woman

Tearing up old friends who can't defend themselves

Saying they're whores

Saying they earnt their money on their backs

Then saying how rich they are

In the cheapest pub in town

I AM A WHOLE LOAD OF NOTHING

My pub

Feminism is a never ending battle

Worth fighting

I wish people would stop stabbing

Each other in the back

Life's hard enough

I try not to judge

Some people can't help themselves

I can't help them

You probably can't help them

Or me

People have tried

Lovers, brother, mothers

I've burnt a lot of people

In my furnace of fears

This one's for all of you

It's the trying

That matters

Not the winning

Winnings for losers

www.ingramcontent.com/pod-product-compliance
Lightning Source LLC
Chambersburg PA
CBHW071324040426
42444CB00009B/2079